JEDI BATTLES

LONDON, NEW YORK, MUNICH,
MELBOURNE, AND DELHI

Editors Lisa Stock, Julia March, Pamela Afram,
Hannah Dolan, Rahul Ganguly, Emma Grange
Senior Editor Victoria Taylor
Designers Owen Bennett, Richard Horsford,
Toby Truphet, Suzena Sengupta
Senior Designer Lisa Sodeau
Pre-Production Producer Marc Staples
Producer Danielle Smith
Managing Editor Laura Gilbert
Design Manager Maxine Pedliham
Publishing Manager Julie Ferris
Art Director Ron Stobbart
Publishing Director Simon Beecroft

Reading Consultant Maureen Fernandes

For Lucasfilm
Executive Editor Jonathan W. Rinzler
Art Director Troy Alders
Keeper of the Holocron Leland Chee
Director of Publishing Carol Roeder

First published in Great Britain in 2014 by
Dorling Kindersley Limited
80 Strand, London, WC2R 0RL

14 15 16 17 10 9 8 7 6 5 4 3 2 1
001–197322–Jan/14

A CIP catalogue record for this book is
available from the British Library.

ISBN: 978-1-40934-680-7

Colour reproduction by Alta Image
Printed and bound in China by South China

Discover more at
www.dk.com
www.starwars.com

Contents

JEDI
TIMELINE

This timeline outlines the main battles and events that have affected the Jedi. Time in the galaxy is fixed around the Battle of Yavin.

KEY
BBY: Before the Battle of Yavin
ABY: After the Battle of Yavin

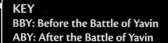

41 BBY: Birth of Anakin | 32 BBY: Battle of Naboo | 22 BBY: Battle of Geonosis

50 BBY **40 BBY** **30 BBY** **20**

REPUBLIC ERA

THE CLONE WARS

0 Battle of Yavin   3 ABY: Battle of Hoth

2 BBY: Rebel   4 ABY: Battle of Endor
Alliance is founded

10 BBY   **0**   **10 ABY**   **20 ABY**

EMPIRE ERA   NEW REPUBLIC ERA

5

Galactic Crisis

In a galaxy far, far away, a great and peaceful Republic existed. It was governed by the Senate – a group of representatives from each planet in the Republic. The representatives, called senators, met in a Senate building on the capital planet of Coruscant. Strong Jedi Knights kept the peace in the Republic.

The Jedi tried to ensure that planets sorted out any arguments by peaceful negotiation. They used a mysterious energy called the Force, and carried glowing lightsabers to defend themselves when negotiation failed.

Sadly, peace in the Republic would be destroyed. A greedy business organisation called the Trade Federation had created an army of machine-soldiers called battle droids. They began to invade planets, starting with a small world called Naboo. As the conflict grew, the Republic had to deploy a massive army to defend itself. War soon erupted in the galaxy.

But all was not what it seemed. Both sides would discover that they had been manipulated by an evil Sith Lord named Darth Sidious who wanted to destroy the Jedi and rule the galaxy!

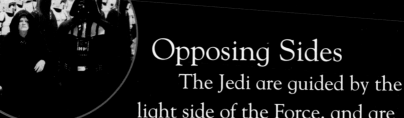

Opposing Sides

The Jedi are guided by the light side of the Force, and are known for their mercy, honesty and compassion. There is also a dark side of the Force. Those who are drawn to it are evil beings named the Sith.

Long ago, the Sith were powerful dark side warriors. However, the Jedi defeated them and they were thought to be extinct. In reality, the Sith were in hiding, waiting for the right moment to return and wreak terror on the Jedi.

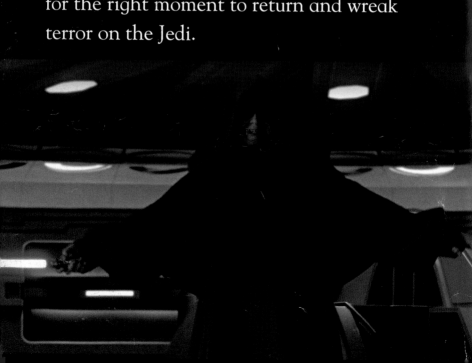

Sith Lord Darth
Sidious was secretly in
control of the Trade
Federation, which
was run by greedy
Neimoidian aliens.
He wanted the
organisation to start a
war that would put

him in power as Emperor and force every
planet to obey him. For years Sidious had kept
his Sith identity and his master plan secret,
fooling everyone by pretending to be a kindly
politician named Senator Palpatine.

Palpatine used his position in the Senate
to manipulate the other planet leaders,
tricking his way into becoming Supreme
Chancellor. Only a brave and determined few
– with the Jedi among them – would refuse to
accept Palpatine's evil rule. They had to
be prepared to fight many epic battles if they
were to bring peace and justice to the galaxy.

Jedi Training

The Jedi Order is an ancient peacekeeping organisation. All Jedi have to learn to live by the Jedi Code – a set of rules that they must obey. According to the Code, the Jedi must use the Force for good. They should have compassion for every form of life, and should engage in combat only to defend others or themselves.

It takes years to become a Jedi Knight and so training usually begins at a very early age. In order to follow the Code it is important that young Jedi, known as Younglings, learn to remain calm and focused in stressful situations. Younglings are taught to use lightsabers as well as techniques for fighting skillfully in a duel. At times their eyes are covered while they train; that way they can learn to feel the Force and use their instincts, instead of relying on what they can see.

Older trainees, called Padawans, also learn how to use the Force to move objects without touching them. A Force pull enables Jedi to bring something to them. A Force push is a powerful technique that repels objects or opponents. To help them in battle, Jedi must also learn to be physically strong, fit and agile.

THE LIFE OF A JEDI

It takes years of hard work to become a full-fledged Jedi. Trainees undergo difficult tests under the watchful eye of a skilled Master of the Force.

JEDI HIGH COUNCIL

The Council is made up of 12 of the greatest Jedi Masters. They resolve disputes, make decisions and uphold the Jedi Code.

YOUNGLING

Those who show Force potential are selected by the Council to begin Jedi training. The Younglings are taken to the Jedi Temple, where they live while studying the basics of the Force.

Grand Master Yoda

GRAND MASTER

A Jedi Master must be exceptional to reach this rank. As Grand Master, Yoda was head of the whole Jedi Order.

*Padawan
Anakin Skywalker*

JEDI TRIALS
When a Master thinks the Youngling has finished their training they will sit the gruelling Jedi Trials.

PADAWAN
If a Youngling works hard, they will be selected by a Jedi to be their Padawan. The Jedi becomes the Padawan's Master and the pair will travel together and carry out one-to-one training.

*Jedi Knight
Aayla
Secura*

JEDI KNIGHT
Those who pass the Trials become qualified Jedi Knights. They can go on their own missions and even train their own Padawan.

*Jedi Master
Luminara
Unduli*

JEDI MASTER
Once a Jedi Knight has trained a Padawan, they can be promoted to Jedi Master. If they show great skill and devotion, they may be invited to sit on the Jedi High Council.

The Lightsaber

Since ancient times, the lightsaber has been the chosen weapon of the Jedi Knights. The user must be experienced in the ways of the Force in order to wield it skillfully in combat.

A lightsaber is held like a sword but instead of a metal blade, a lightsaber has a beam of energy that bursts from the handle when the weapon is ignited. Lightsabers can easily cut through the

toughest of material – even metal doors –
but not the blade of another lightsaber.
The powerful lightsaber has other important
uses in combat. Jedi can use the Force to
predict incoming energy bolts from blaster
guns and then use a lightsaber to deflect
the bolts back toward their opponent.

The Sith also use lightsabers in combat.
Sometimes their weapons are even
double-bladed, which suits their aggressive
style of fighting.

TOOLS OF
THE TRADE

A Jedi does not require many tools. Everything they need is carried in a utility belt, which also holds their lightsaber. They wear simple clothes and tough boots for missions and battles.

COMLINK

A security-enhanced comlink is used to talk to other Jedi. Its encoders ensure messages cannot be intercepted.

LIGHTSABER

All Jedi lightsabers follow a similar design. Each Jedi builds their own lightsaber to complement their fighting technique.

HOLOPROJECTOR

This device can send and receive secure 3-D holotransmissions via a comlink to be viewed in real time.

Lightsaber
blade

Simple Jedi
tunic

Lightsaber
hilt

Tools held
in belt

Trousers
designed for
combat

Practical
travel
boots

Sith Methods

Like the Jedi, the Sith are able to sense and use the Force. However, the Sith's Force training varies greatly from that of the Jedi. They use the dark side of the Force and gain their power from raw emotions such as anger and hatred. The Sith do not value life or feel compassion, and their ferocious style of combat reflects their violent attitudes.

The Sith act in aggression and not in defence, and are prepared to do anything in battle – no matter how devious.

The Sith always come in pairs – a Master and an apprentice. Knowledge of the dark side of the Force is passed on from Master to apprentice.

The Sith can use the Force to produce lethal Force lightning. They channel the Force through their bodies and discharge powerful bolts of energy from their palms and fingertips into their opponents.

The Sith can also channel the power of the Force to choke a victim without actually touching them. This deadly combat technique is known as the Force choke.

TWO-FACED

Senator Palpatine was really the most powerful Sith Lord in the galaxy. As a senator, he appeared to be kind and supportive – but as the leader of the Sith, he was evil and hungry for power.

"There is no civility, only politics."

Senator Palpatine

SENATOR PALPATINE
Senator Palpatine received praise from the Jedi Order for his wisdom. The Jedi were unaware that he was controlling the Senate for his own good.

> **"Only through me can you achieve a power greater than any Jedi. Learn to know the dark side of the Force."**

Darth Sidious

DARTH SIDIOUS
As Sith Lord Darth Sidious, Palpatine ruled over his subjects with fear. But he always concealed his face, so that no one could discover his secret.

LAND BATTLES
Soldiers must be prepared for combat on a rough and varied terrain. Troops utilise specialised vehicles and artillery, and must stay alert in case of sudden attacks.

Grass Plains Battle

Even the most peaceful species will fight to defend their planet.

The Gungans were a water-dwelling species who lived on Naboo, a planet of swamps and grasslands. They were known for avoiding contact with the Naboo people and their dislike of conflict. That was before the Trade Federation invaded Naboo with an army of battle droids, under the secret orders of Darth Sidious. With their planet at stake, the Gungans were forced to take up arms and work with the Naboo people and the Jedi.

The Gungans had not raised an army for over a hundred years, but they did not falter. Their job was to lure the droid forces away from the Naboo

capital, Theed, so that the Jedi could move in and fight the Trade Federation there.

The scene of the battle was an area named the Great Grass Plains. Assembled on the plains, the Gungan Grand Army faced a massive army of battle droids, which were being controlled by a Trade Federation spaceship. It was a scary sight! Would the Gungans' battle skills be enough to compete?

Gungan battle tactics relied heavily on defence. They chose battle sites near swamps, so that if they retreated their foes could not follow. On the battlefield their first move was to deploy huge energy shields. The shields were activated by machines carried on the

backs of giant swamp lizards named fambaas. These energy shields were great for protecting armies from enemy missiles, but on the Great Grass Plains the Gungans

discovered that they had a serious weakness.
Battle droids could walk right through them!

Under fire from droid blasters, the Gungans
responded with their traditional weapons –
plasma balls filled with explosive energy, which
they hurled into the air with catapults and
throwing sticks. Glowing, handheld energy
shields protected them against blaster bolts.

The Gungans could not defeat all the battle
droids, but they hoped to engage them long
enough for their Jedi allies to strike elsewhere.
Their strategy was successful! Out in space, a
Naboo pilot blew up the Droid Control Ship,
and the battle droids were stopped in their tracks.

WHO ARE THE GUNGANS?

This swamp-dwelling race lives in the underwater city of Otoh Gunga, located deep within Lake Paonga on Naboo. Though a peaceful race, Gungans are capable of combat, and use plasma-based weapons in battle.

OTOH GUNGA
Otoh Gunga is made up of a cluster of giant bubbles held together by special machines.

Jar Jar Binks

This clumsy Gungan once lived in a swamp near Otoh Gunga. Jar Jar became good friends with Jedi Master Qui-Gon Jinn.

WHO RULES THE GUNGANS?

Boss Nass is the ruler of Otoh Gunga. When Separatists attacked Naboo, he assembled a massive army from Gungan settlements to fight the enemy.

Battle of Geonosis

To battle its enemies' huge droid armies, the Republic recruited a ready-made army of its own. It was made up of millions of clone troopers, all identical copies of a single ultimate soldier.

The clone army first saw action on the planet of Geonosis, in a battle that would force Jedi Master Yoda to become a military general against his peaceful instincts.

Jedi Obi-Wan Kenobi and Anakin Skywalker had been captured by the Separatists and faced execution in an arena on Geonosis along with Senator Padmé Amidala of Naboo. When a Jedi rescue attempt was initiated, the Separatists unleashed hordes of super battle droids in the arena. Could the clone army stop these droids and save the Jedi? Led by Master Yoda, the clones came to the rescue. A massive battle ensued – one that soon spread outside the arena. Many Jedi and clones were destroyed, but eventually the droids retreated. The Battle of Geonosis was the first conflict in what later became known as the Clone Wars.

SEPARATIST
DROIDS

Big corporations like the Trade Federation supplied the money to build the droid army for the Separatists. The Separatists used these unrelenting soldiers to fight their battles.

DROIDEKA
Droidekas are fast, deadly destroyer droids. They attack by curling into a wheel shape and rolling at their enemies with terrifying speed.

Twin blaster cannons

HAILFIRE DROID

Hailfire droids are armed with two racks of deadly missiles. Enemies who avoid these may be crushed under their enormous wheels.

Laser cannon

Two missile launchers

Fragile construction

Thick armour

Built-in laser cannon

SUPER BATTLE DROID

These droids are bigger, tougher versions of regular battle droids. They carry more powerful weapons, and are harder to destroy.

BATTLE DROID

These droid soldiers are programmed to blindly obey orders. Cheap and expendable, they are produced by the million.

SPIDER DROID

Spider droids come in many forms. They range from burrowing dwarf types to homing spider droids who stalk the battlefields on long, extendable legs.

Heavy blaster cannon

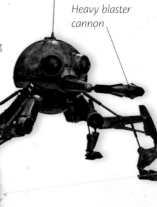

Can cross rough ground

Battle of Kashyyyk

One of the biggest battles of the Clone Wars – and also one of the biggest turning points – took place on Kashyyyk. This thickly forested planet was home to tall, furry creatures called Wookiees, who were firm allies of the Republic. The Wookiees fought bravely alongside the clone troopers, battling the Separatist tanks and droids on land and on water. Victory on Kashyyyk seemed certain, but then disaster struck.

Chancellor Palpatine had secretly brainwashed the clone troopers to switch sides when they received a signal called

Order 66. When this signal was given, clones everywhere turned their weapons on their Jedi generals. Nearly all the Jedi leaders were killed, although Yoda escaped with the help of brave Wookiee chieftain Tarfful.

The clones obeyed only Sith orders now, and when Darth Sidious became Emperor he made them his personal army – the dreaded stormtroopers. The Empire was born!

Battle of Hoth

The Empire ruled the galaxy with an iron grip, but many brave people struggled to overthrow it. They were known as the Rebel Alliance, and Emperor Palpatine and Sith Lord Darth Vader directed much of the Empire's military strength toward crushing them.

The rebels operated out of a secret base in a converted ice cave on the frozen planet of Hoth. When Darth Vader discovered the base, he attacked it with great force. The battle that followed left the rebel cause reeling.

Central to the Empire's attack were AT-ATs – giant walking tanks armed with blasters. The rebels could not stop these monstrous tanks with their guns and lasers. Although the rebels brought down two of them in a daring manoeuvre using trip cables, they were finally forced to flee, leaving their base to Darth Vader and his stormtroopers.

The Battle of Hoth was a disaster for the rebels, but it was not the end. Pilot Han Solo escaped in his spaceship, the *Millennium Falcon*, with Princess Leia, C-3PO and Chewbacca.

CLONE TROOPER TO
STORMTROOPER

Clone troopers of the Galactic Republic were constantly upgraded with better armour and equipment. When Palpatine built the Empire, the clones got their biggest change of all. Transformed into Imperial stormtroopers, they were given brand-new armour, and a brand-new role – destroying the Emperor's enemies.

Helmet design based on Jango Fett's helmet

DC-15A blaster rifle

Armour made up of 20 separate pieces

PHASE 1: CLONE TROOPER
Troopers of the Republic Army initially wore identical white armour that was bulky and uncomfortable.

New helmet with air filters and targeting systems

Helmet upgraded with emergency air supply

Powerful E-11 blaster rifle

DC-15A still in use, as well as grenades

Improved armour could survive

Armour pieces reduced to 18

PHASE 2: STORMTROOPER
Stronger, more flexible armour was worn by the clone troopers who became the first stormtroopers.

IMPERIAL STORMTROOPER
The final version of the Imperial stormtrooper armour had fewer individual pieces, to aid efficiency.

Battle of Endor

Even the craftiest schemes can go wrong!

Emperor Palpatine hatched a plot to draw the Rebel Alliance out from hiding. He knew they would attempt to destroy the shield generator on the forest moon of Endor, which protected his massive battle station, named the Death Star. When a rebel team led by Luke Skywalker, Princess Leia, Han Solo and the Wookiee ally named Chewbacca landed on Endor the Imperial army was ready for them. But it was not ready for their allies – furry creatures called Ewoks.

The little Ewoks took the stormtroopers by surprise. They did not have sophisticated weapons, but they knew how to fight in a forest, hurling rocks at the stormtroopers, leaving them in disarray. The rebels were able to destroy the shield generator, allowing their space fleet to attack the Death Star in a battle that would signal the end of the Empire.

SPACE BATTLES

Pilots face great danger in space battles, as they can be attacked from all sides. They need to show bravery as well as skill and, in most cases, experience helps.

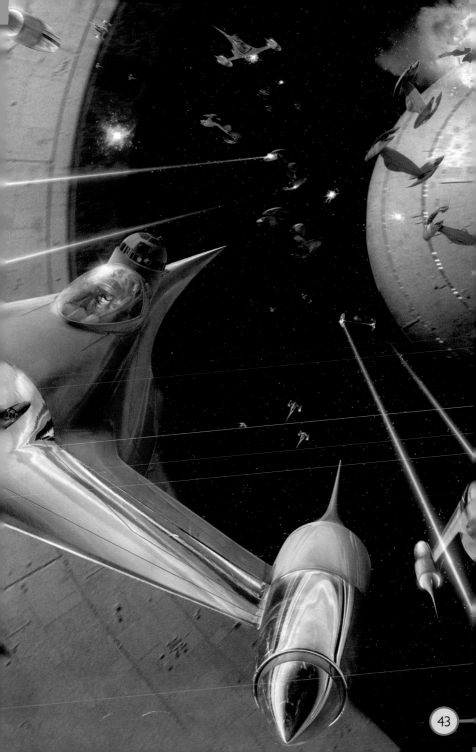

Naboo Space Battle

When the native people of
Naboo entered battle with the
evil Trade Federation, starfighters
were their best spacecraft for the space-based
part of the conflict. The ships are
aerodynamic, agile and fast. In defence,
the Trade Federation's ring-shaped Droid
Control Ship unleashed deadly vulture droid
ships on the starfighters.

An experienced pilot is usually essential,
but one of the starfighter pilots was a
nine-year-old boy named Anakin Skywalker.
He was hiding in a starfighter that was
docked on Naboo when the spacecraft
accidentally took off into space.

Bravery is required by the Jedi in any type of conflict and when caught up in a dangerous space battle, young Anakin showed a natural boldness. He was able to enter the Droid Control Ship, avoiding deadly laser blasts, and fire torpedoes into its reactor. Anakin escaped when the massive ship exploded. The ship had sent signals to every battle droid on Naboo. Droids only follow orders, so as the Control Ship was destroyed, they automatically stopped functioning.

SPACECRAFT FACT FILE

In space fights, spacecraft of various shapes and sizes engage in battle. The Separatists and the Empire employed anything from tiny droids to massive Star Destroyers to fight off their enemies in space, but the Jedi prefered flying smaller starfighters.

.... *Solar arrays*

Hull protected by shield generators

TIE FIGHTER
Length: 9 m (29 ft)
Weapons: Laser cannons
Built by: Sienar Fleet Systems

SLAVE I
Length: 21.15 m (95.75 ft)
Weapons: Laser cannons, ion cannons
Built by: Kuat Systems Engineering

.... *Heavily armoured*

Shiny chromium finish ....

NABOO J-TYPE BARGE
Length: 39 m (128 ft)
Weapons: None
Built by: Theed Palace Space Vessel Engineering Corps

Droids starfighters do not require pilots ......

IMPERIAL STAR DESTROYER
Length: 1,600 m (5,249 ft)
Weapons: Turbolaser batteries, heavy ion cannons
Built by: Kuat Drive Yards

VULTURE DROID
Length: 6.96 m (22.7 ft)
Weapons: Laser cannon, energy torpedoes
Built by: Xi Char Cathedral Factories

Can carry several starfighters

Space for one pilot ....

ETA-2 ACTIS STARFIGHTER
Length: 5.47 m (17.94 ft)
Weapons: Laser cannons, seismic mines, torpedoes
Built by: Kuat Systems Engineering

DELTA-7B STARFIGHTER
Length: 8 m (26.2 ft)
Weapons: Laser cannons
Built by: Kuat Systems Engineering

.... Can hold a Jedi and an astromech droid

The Clone Wars

Some space battles
involve two ships in a duel,
which is known as a dogfight.
In others, many different ships do battle
with each other.

When full-scale war broke out between
the Republic and the Separatist droid army,
there was a spectacular space conflict above
the planet Coruscant, home of the Jedi
Temple. Separatist droid fighters engaged
Republic starfighters, while each side's huge
warships blasted away at each other. Both
sides lost many vessels in the dramatic and
explosive battle.

Obi-Wan Kenobi and Anakin Skywalker
had gained a reputation as the best pilots in
the galaxy, but they still struggled with the
sheer number of ships trying to destroy them.

They piloted their fast Interceptor
starfighters, dodging enemy fire together
with extreme skill. But they faced many

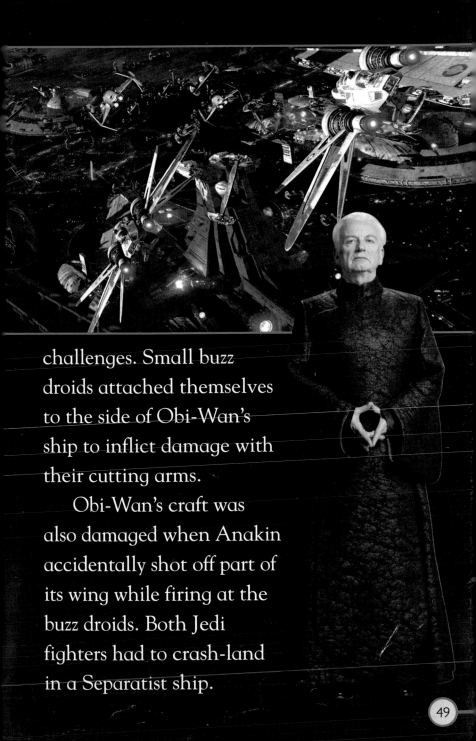

challenges. Small buzz
droids attached themselves
to the side of Obi-Wan's
ship to inflict damage with
their cutting arms.

Obi-Wan's craft was
also damaged when Anakin
accidentally shot off part of
its wing while firing at the
buzz droids. Both Jedi
fighters had to crash-land
in a Separatist ship.

Rebel Ship

Rebel Han Solo's ship, the
Millennium Falcon, was deployed
in many dogfights across the galaxy.
Though the *Falcon* was heavily battle-
scarred from its many space adventures, it
could still outmanoeuvre most enemy craft.
In a tricky situation, the *Falcon* made the
jump to hyperspace. This allowed the ship
to vanish and reappear somewhere far away.

When Vader's Star Destroyer spaceship
was on Han Solo's tail and determined to
catch him, the *Falcon*'s hyperspace drive had
been damaged. Luckily, Han was an expert
pilot and a quick thinker. He headed into a
dangerous asteroid field, knowing that he
could find a temporary hiding place there.
His piloting skills allowed him to weave his
ship in between the space rocks, coming to
rest in an asteroid crater. Unfortunately, Han
found that his hiding place wasn't actually a
crater. It was the belly of an enormous space

slug. Han raced his ship out of the asteroid
field and landed in the only place where the
Falcon could evade radar detection – on a
tower of the Star Destroyer. His plan worked.
He waited until the Star Destroyer emitted
its space waste and allowed the *Falcon* to
float away with the rest of the waste. The
Millennium Falcon had escaped undetected
by the Imperial fleet.

INSIDE THE
MILLENNIUM
FALCON

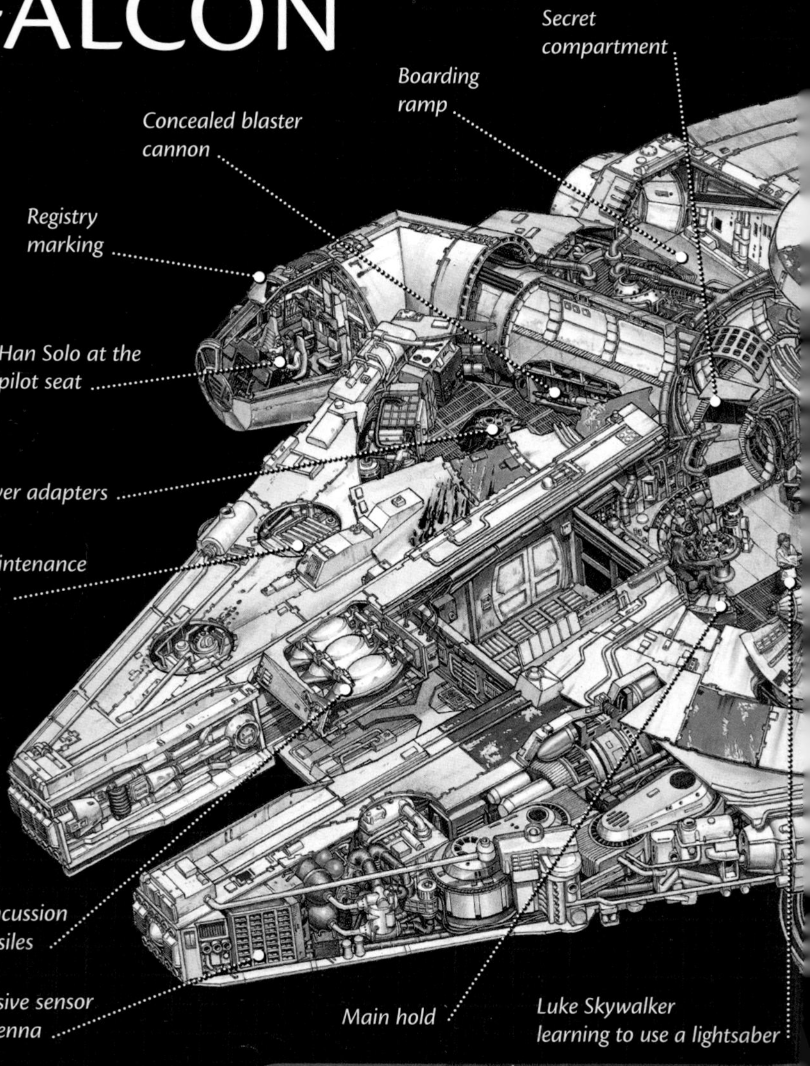

Secret
compartment

Boarding
ramp

Concealed blaster
cannon

Registry
marking

Han Solo at the
pilot seat

Power adapters

Maintenance
bay

Concussion
missiles

Passive sensor
antenna

Main hold

Luke Skywalker
learning to use a lightsaber

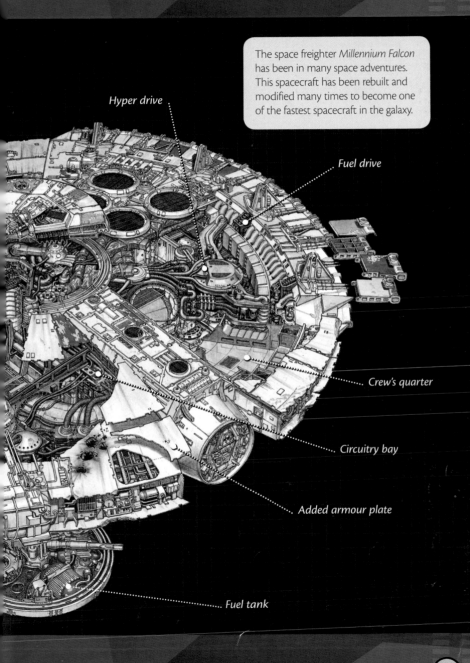

The space freighter *Millennium Falcon* has been in many space adventures. This spacecraft has been rebuilt and modified many times to become one of the fastest spacecraft in the galaxy.

Hyper drive

Fuel drive

Crew's quarter

Circuitry bay

Added armour plate

Fuel tank

THE FIRST
DEATH STAR

Darth Sidious wanted to create a physical symbol of his immense power. He ordered the construction of a huge, mobile battle station named the Death Star, which had enough firepower to destroy an entire planet.

Main power generator

DEATH STAR I
The station was the size of a moon and was divided into two hemispheres. There was a wide trench around its equator.

Hypermatter reactor

Central computer core

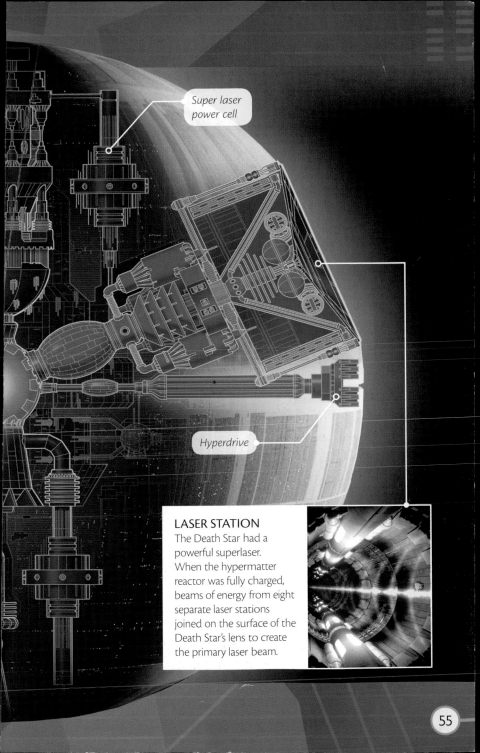

Super laser
power cell

Hyperdrive

LASER STATION
The Death Star had a
powerful superlaser.
When the hypermatter
reactor was fully charged,
beams of energy from eight
separate laser stations
joined on the surface of the
Death Star's lens to create
the primary laser beam.

Death Star Attack

The Rebel Alliance was dedicated to opposing the oppressive rule of the Galactic Empire, even though they were desperately under-equipped. The Empire had a massive starfleet, but the Alliance made do with a small number of battle-worn starfighters.

However, the rebels discovered an advantage when they stole secret plans from the Death Star. The plans revealed a flaw: if a starfighter could fire a torpedo into a tiny exhaust port, the chain reaction would destroy the entire battle station.

Rebel pilots used X-wing and Y-wing starfighters from their base on the planet Yavin 4 to launch a space assault on the Death Star.

The Empire was not expecting such small fighters to attack its deadly superweapon, and the rebel squads took advantage of this vital element of surprise. Rebel pilot Luke Skywalker was focused and skilled enough to strike the target. Chased by Imperial ships, Luke fired at the exhaust port that led into the heart of the battle station's reactor. The Death Star exploded, and the rebels scored their first major victory against the Empire.

THE SECOND
DEATH STAR

The second Death Star was even bigger
and more powerful than the first. Here
are some of the battle station's features.

*More
powerful
and
accurate
superlaser*

*Equatorial
trench*

HANGAR
The Imperial engineers
allocated more hangar space
in the Death Star II so it
could carry more droids.

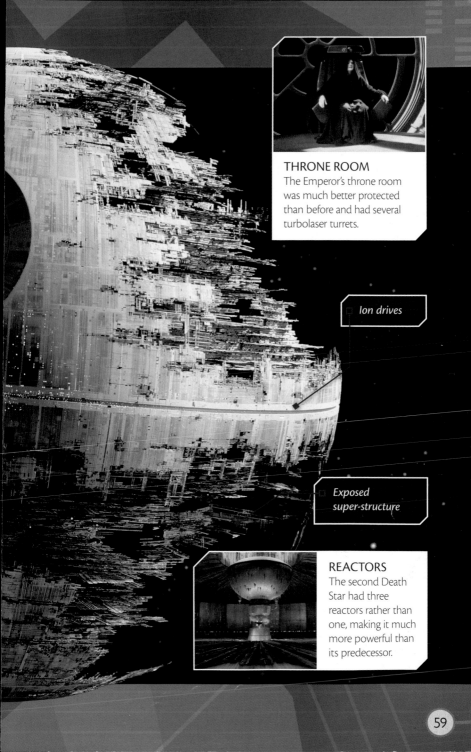

THRONE ROOM

The Emperor's throne room was much better protected than before and had several turbolaser turrets.

Ion drives

Exposed super-structure

REACTORS

The second Death Star had three reactors rather than one, making it much more powerful than its predecessor.

T-65 X-WING
STARFIGHTER

This long, narrow starship boasts excellent power, balance and stability. After Luke Skywalker piloted his X-wing to destroy the first Death Star, it became a symbol of the Rebel Alliance.

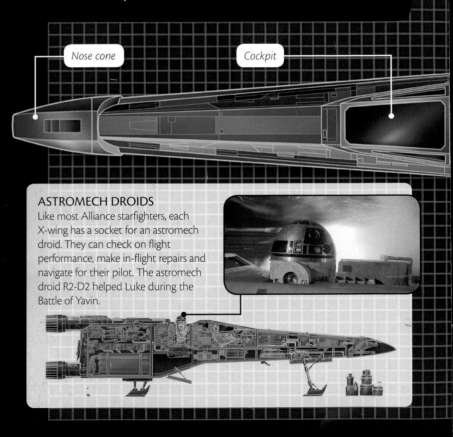

Nose cone

Cockpit

ASTROMECH DROIDS
Like most Alliance starfighters, each X-wing has a socket for an astromech droid. They can check on flight performance, make in-flight repairs and navigate for their pilot. The astromech droid R2-D2 helped Luke during the Battle of Yavin.

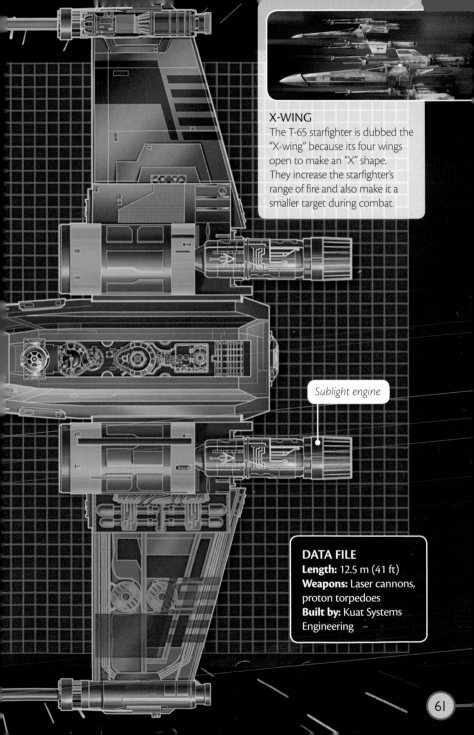

X-WING

The T-65 starfighter is dubbed the "X-wing" because its four wings open to make an "X" shape. They increase the starfighter's range of fire and also make it a smaller target during combat.

Sublight engine

DATA FILE
Length: 12.5 m (41 ft)
Weapons: Laser cannons, proton torpedoes
Built by: Kuat Systems Engineering

Final Space Battle

The last fight between the
rebels and the Galactic Empire
was a space battle. The entire rebel
fleet came out of hiding to launch a carefully
planned assault on the second Death Star.

While the rebels worked to deactivate
the Death Star's energy defence shield on
Endor, their fleet focused its attack on the
Empire's massive Star Destroyer battleships.
The rebel fleet consisted of A-wing, B-wing
and X-wing starfighters, which were able to
manoeuvre easily around the Star Destroyers
– but they were still at risk from the Death
Star's deadly destroyer beam.

The battle turned when the rebel team
on Endor succeeded in deactivating the
Death Star's defence shield. A brave rebel
pilot named Landó Calrissian was able to fly
the *Millennium Falcon* into the Death Star's
core and detonate the battle station's power
plant. The resulting explosion destroyed the
Death Star. The rebels had finally defeated
the Galactic Empire.

LIGHTSABER CLASHES

In lightsaber combat, size doesn't matter. Regardless of a warrior's stature, if they have strength, dexterity and are attuned to the Force, they will have the power to defeat any opponent.

Duel on Naboo

In a lightsaber duel, confidence is always a good thing. But when confidence turns to arrogance, the duellist can easily throw away what seems to be a certain victory.

Sith Lord Darth Maul was so sure of his skills that he believed he could defeat two Jedi at once. When Maul battled Qui-Gon Jinn and Obi-Wan Kenobi at the same time

on Naboo, at first it seemed he was right. Thanks to his mastery of martial arts and his deadly saberstaff, Darth Maul was a fearsome opponent for the Jedi. Qui-Gon was fatally injured in the clash, and although Obi-Wan fought on bravely, it was clear that the Sith was more powerful.

Maul's Force push left Obi-Wan hanging from a pipe, having lost his lightsaber, and it looked as if Maul would finish off the Jedi. But his arrogance got the better of him. He stopped for a moment to taunt his opponent. Obi-Wan summoned all of his strength and used the Force to retrieve Qui-Gon's weapon, defeating Maul with one blow. Darth Maul was destroyed, a victim of his own arrogance.

HOW TO BUILD A
LIGHTSABER

Each lightsaber is made to suit its owner's needs and preferences. Lightsabers consist of a handle – called the hilt – that emits a blade of powerful energy. Special parts allow the power and length of the lightsaber blade to be changed.

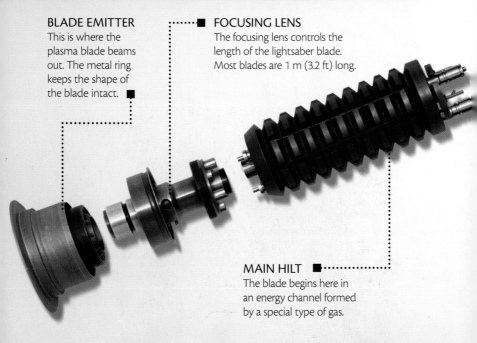

BLADE EMITTER
This is where the plasma blade beams out. The metal ring keeps the shape of the blade intact. ■

■ FOCUSING LENS
The focusing lens controls the length of the lightsaber blade. Most blades are 1 m (3.2 ft) long.

MAIN HILT ■
The blade begins here in an energy channel formed by a special type of gas.

CONTROLS

Buttons and switches activate the blade, but Jedi who are skilled in the Force can control the blade using the Force alone.

POWER CELL

Energy from special diatium batteries heats up gas to create plasma for the blade. ■

POMMEL CAP ■

The pommel seals the end of the lightsaber. It may often contain a backup battery.

Crystal

At the heart of every lightsaber hilt is a crystal that needs to be placed carefully in order to work. Jedi lightsaber crystals are mined from the planet Ilum. The Sith use artificial crystals that make their lightsabers glow red.

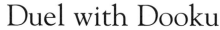

Duel with Dooku

The Jedi train long and hard to ensure that they always keep their cool in battle. For hot-headed young Jedi apprentice Anakin Skywalker, this skill was particularly hard to master. Anakin's impatience proved to be disastrous when he and Obi-Wan were sent to capture Sith Apprentice Count Dooku on the rocky planet of Geonosis.

Dooku was once a Jedi Master but his independent spirit led him away from the order. Now he used his formidable lightsaber skills against the Jedi. As a more experienced fighter,

Obi-Wan knew that it would be better to coordinate their attack, but Anakin was too impatient to listen to his Master.

Anakin rushed toward Dooku, who used Force lightning to send Anakin crashing against a wall. Anakin's initial mistake had given the Sith Lord a great advantage. Dooku was a master swordsman who excelled in lightsaber combat and he made Anakin pay dearly for his error. In one swift blow the cruel Sith sliced off Anakin's right forearm!

Battle on Utapau

An opponent armed with one lightsaber is a challenge for the Jedi to face. A foe armed with four lightsabers is definitely not to be underestimated! Supreme Commander of the Separatist Army, General Grievous, was a powerful military leader until he was injured in a shuttle crash. He was rebuilt as a cyborg with four artificial arms that allowed him to wield four lightsabers at once. Despite his lightsaber training, Grievous could not use the Force like the Jedi, but his brute strength and speed made him very difficult to beat in combat.

Grievous liked to steal lightsabers from the Jedi he killed, and he hoped to add Obi-Wan's weapon to his collection!

When the two came face-to-face in one of planet Utapau's large sinkhole cities, Obi-Wan had to contend with many unpredictable attacks from the half-machine, half-creature. However, without the power of the Force, Grievous was no match for the Jedi. Obi-Wan was able to anticipate Grievous's blows and cut off several of his hands. The cyborg was forced to flee into outer space, where his tough duranium shell allowed him to withstand the crushing air pressure.

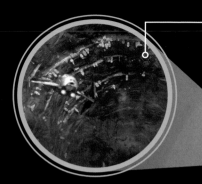

SINKHOLE
Natives live in settlements inside large sinkholes on the planet. Here, they are protected from the harsh surface winds.

PLANET SURFACE
The surface of Utapau is dry. Few plants grow here. Harsh winds sweep the planet at all times.

WELCOME TO
UTAPAU

Utapau was a peaceful planet before General Grievous and Obi-Wan's fierce battle there. Located on the Outer Rim of the galaxy, the planet and its natives had hoped to remain neutral in the battle of the Clone Wars.

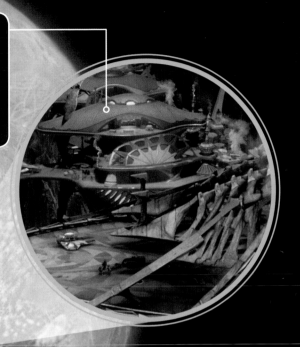

PAU CITY
Located in a large sinkhole, Pau City serves as a spaceport for visitors. It also has repair and refuelling facilities for spacecraft landing on the planet.

Natives
Utapau is inhabited by two native species. The tall, gray Pau'ans carry out trade and commerce. The short, stocky Utai serve as the planet's labour force.

Pau'an

Utai

Master and Apprentice

Obi-Wan Kenobi was used to fighting fierce lightsaber duels with merciless Sith foes, but never before had he fought against a friend.

From the moment a distraught Obi-Wan learned that his Padawan, Anakin Skywalker, had become a Sith called Darth Vader, a confrontation was inevitable.

Obi-Wan faced Vader on the volcano planet of Mustafar in a dangerous lava mining facility. Obi-Wan tried to reason with him, but it was clear that Anakin had been lost to the dark side. Now transformed from friends to foes, Vader and Obi-Wan ignited their lightsabers and began an intense battle above the flaming lava. Obi-Wan had taught Anakin

well and both fighters were now evenly
matched in strength and skill. Having
fought as a team countless times before,
the two men knew each other's best moves
– and weaknesses. In the end, Obi-Wan's
experience helped him to deal a winning
blow. Vader was defeated ... but not for long.

ANAKIN SKYWALKER: TROUBLED JEDI

THE LIGHT SIDE
Before turning to the dark side, Anakin had the potential to become a great Jedi. Many Jedi had faith in him, but he struggled to control his emotions in the way a Jedi should.

"The Force is unusually strong with him."
QUI-GON JINN

"There's something about this boy."
QUI-GON JINN

"He will not let me down."
OBI-WAN KENOBI

THE DARK SIDE

Anakin was not able to overcome his negative emotions. He was goaded by Palpatine, who exploited his feelings of anxiety and frustration. Anakin turned to the dark side.

"They don't trust you, Anakin."

PALPATINE

"Be careful of the Jedi, Anakin."

PALPATINE

"Learn the power of the dark side, Anakin."

PALPATINE

79

Close Contest

When the most powerful Jedi battled against the most powerful Sith, the two sides of the Force clashed in spectacular style. Grand Master Yoda took on Darth Sidious in the Senate building on Coruscant and proved that strength and power have nothing to do with size. The Jedi was much smaller than his Sith opponent, but he used his size and agility to his advantage. Yoda leaped and twirled above Sidious, confusing his enemy and catching him by surprise with skillful lightsaber blows.

The devastating fury of the Sith Lord was matched by Yoda's knowledge of the Force, making the two equally fierce. Using great concentration and focus, Yoda was able to absorb Sidious's brutal Force lightning and deflect it back again.

However, the wise old Jedi realised that he could not defeat Sidious this time. Yoda's size came in handy again as he made a quick exit through a ventilation shaft and escaped to a distant planet called Dagobah.

Death Star Duel

A Jedi must stay true to the Jedi Code, no matter how old he may be. Obi-Wan Kenobi was an elderly man by the time he fought against Darth Vader once again, but his dream of a revived Republic had not weakened. This time their duel took place on board the Emperor's first Death Star.

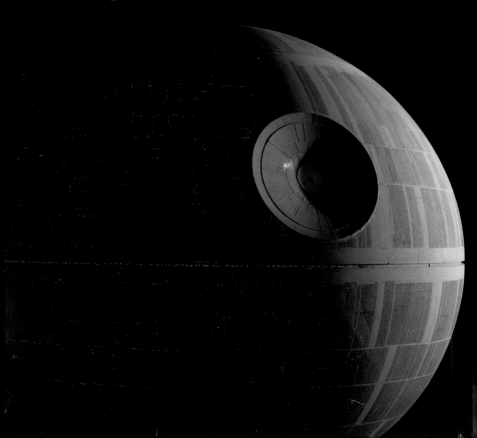

Obi-Wan Kenobi had been in hiding on
Tatooine since the Emperor seized control of the
galaxy. When Rebel Alliance leader Princess
Leia asked for his help to take the secret Death
Star plans to the Rebel Alliance, Obi-Wan
recruited a young farmboy named Luke
Skywalker, who knew he had latent Jedi powers.

Obi-Wan knew
he had to face
Darth Vader
again, but felt it
was the only way
to save Luke and
Princess Leia.
This duel was
very different

from their last. Obi-Wan was older and weaker
while Vader was even stronger, fuelled by hatred
and thirst for revenge. Obi-Wan knew that if he
sacrificed his own life he could save his friends,
so he allowed Vader to destroy him, proving to
be a truly great and selfless Jedi.

MISSING
PRINCESS

Brave senator Princess Leia was taken prisoner for stealing secret plans to the Death Star. Before she was caught, she sent a message to Obi-Wan.

SECRET MESSAGE
Realising she could not escape, Leia entrusted R2-D2 with the Death Star plans and a desperate message for Obi-Wan.

TRANSMISSION
Astromech droid R2-D2 helped fulfill his mission by transmitting Princess Leia's message through a holographic beam.

HIDDEN JEDI
Before Obi-Wan saw Leia's message he had been living in hiding. Now he needed to act immediately – he was her only hope.

Cloud City Clash

As well as being a brave
Rebel Alliance pilot, Luke
Skywalker was a Jedi apprentice.
This adventure-seeking boy from
Tatooine came to Jedi training late in
life, but the Force was strong with him.
He was taught by Obi-Wan Kenobi
and later Yoda became his Master.
Luke's mother was Padmé
Amidala and his father was
Anakin Skywalker, although
Anakin had already turned to
the dark side and become
Darth Vader by the time
Luke discovered who his
parents really were.
    Like his father, Luke
could be impatient
and reckless. Even
though he had
not completed

his training, Luke rushed to Cloud City where he duelled Vader for the first time. Luke did not yet have enough experience to combat Vader's superior Force powers and lightsaber skills. Vader's attack was relentless and in a final blow, the Sith Lord severed Luke's hand.

Luke may have had many similarities to his father but they differed in one key way: despite Vader's best efforts, Luke refused to be corrupted and submit to the dark side.

Lethal Confrontation

Luke Skywalker always tried to see the good in people. He even believed that someone as cruel as his father, Darth Vader, could be saved from the dark side and never gave up hope that he could change.

Luke resisted the temptation of the dark side once again during another lightsaber duel with his father, this time on the second Death Star. Luke showed Vader that the desire for honour and justice was just as strong as the promise of incredible power, which Vader insisted the dark side would bring him.

Father and son were now equally strong
with the Force and equally skilled with their
lightsabers. But this battle was about more
than just physical strength and Force powers.
Their family bond affected their actions – each
man was desperate to recruit the other rather
than destroy him.

Luke's faith in his father was ultimately
rewarded. When Sidious attempted to slay
Luke, Anakin Skywalker was reborn within
Darth Vader and he returned to the light side
of the Force. The balance he destroyed when
he became a Sith 23 years earlier was restored.

EPIC SHOWDOWNS
In the heat of conflict, combatants must rely on great daring, skill and tactical thinking to win the day.

Kamino Conflict

In their battle for peace, the Jedi are often called upon to arrest criminals. Ten years after the victory on Naboo, Obi-Wan travelled to a watery planet called Kamino, in the hunt for a bounty hunter named Jango Fett. The Kaminoans were secretly creating a huge clone trooper army. The clone soldiers were exact copies of Jango, but they grew much faster than a human. This allowed the Kaminoans to quickly produce thousands of soldiers.

The creation of this army was supposedly ordered by a Jedi named Sifo-Dyas, but was actually done without the knowledge of the Jedi High Council, as part

of Darth Sidious's master plan.

Obi-Wan pursued Jango and battled him in a violent brawl. Jango was not a Jedi but his suit was fitted with gadgets and weapons, such as wrist blades, blaster pistols and a jetpack, which gave him an advantage at times over Obi-Wan. During the hand-to-hand combat, Obi-Wan was knocked over the edge of a landing platform. Jango was dragged over, too, but used his secret gadgets to free himself just in time. In this conflict it was the Jedi who was left behind, while Jango escaped on his starship, *Slave I.*

BOUNTY HUNTERS

The galaxy has a thriving trade for bounty hunters like Jango Fett. These hired assassins would destroy anyone for a fee. The Sith often turned to bounty hunters to do their evil deeds.

AURRA SING

Evil Aurra left the Jedi Order to become a bounty hunter.

SPECIES: Near-human
WEAPON: Dual-triggered DX-13 blasters
SPECIALTY: Tracking prey with her sensor implants

JANGO FETT

Raised by a race of warriors, Jango was ruthless in combat.

SPECIES: Human
WEAPON: WESTAR-34 blasters
SPECIALTY: Physical combat

BOSSK

Bossk was vile and mean, and could grow back limbs lost in battle.

SPECIES: Trandoshan
WEAPON: V10 grenade launcher
SPECIALTY: Tough and merciless attitude

BOBA FETT

Boba was trained by his father, Jango Fett, and was a deadly shot.

SPECIES: Human

WEAPON: EE-3 carbine rifle
SPECIALTY: Speedy missions

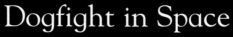

Dogfight in Space

Obi-Wan Kenobi and Jango Fett were equally tactical in battle. Their abilities were put to the test in a one-on-one dogfight deep in space.

Jango's customised spacecraft, *Slave I*, was one of the deadliest ships in the galaxy. It was armed with powerful weapons and lethal surprises. Jango's son, Boba, travelled in *Slave I* with his father, learning from his every action.

Piloting his Delta-7 starfighter, Obi-Wan chased Jango into a dangerous asteroid field. Any collision with these rocks would be fatal. Knowing this, Jango set off massive explosions that blasted rocks at the Jedi's ship. Obi-Wan may not have liked flying, but he was a skilled pilot, and he

dodged each explosion. Jango's weapons
were far superior to Obi-Wan's. He fired a
seeker missile – which locks on to its target.
Obi-Wan escaped the missile and faked his
ship's explosion, leading Jango to believe
that Obi-Wan had been destroyed. The
clever Jedi had decided to bide his time, and
was hiding on one of the asteroids, meaning
no-one was victorious in this epic showdown.

STARFIGHTER
ESCAPE

Obi-Wan Kenobi's Delta-7 starfighter has a streamlined design, the ability to reach fast speeds and excellent manoeuvrability – perfect for trying to escape a determined bounty hunter.

POWER
Equipped with two duel laser cannons, Obi-Wan's ship had the capability to unleash a withering frontal assault.

DESIGN
The sleek, blade-like form afforded excellent visibility, especially in forward and lateral directions.

COMMUNICATION
In an emergency, Kenobi's ship could relay encrypted signals in order to communicate with other Jedi.

DEFENCE
This ultra-light fighter was well shielded against impacts and blasts.

STEALTH
The tiny profile made it difficult to detect and easy to hide from long-ranged sensors.

DROID HELP
An astromech droid called R4-P17 sat in the starfighter. It helped Obi-Wan escape the deadly missile.

Beastly Battle

The Jedi have faced many fearsome opponents, but none quite so gruesome and savage as the beasts on the planet Geonosis.

Obi-Wan, Anakin and Padmé Amidala were sentenced to public execution by wild beasts in a huge arena. As Geonosians watched from the stands, three deadly creatures were let loose and set upon the human prisoners. Each one was bigger and uglier than the last! The bloodthirsty acklay walked on three pairs of giant bony claws. The reek had pointed horns on its head for

goring opponents. The nexu had a mouthful of sharp fangs that it bared in anticipation of fresh meat. It looked like there was no way out!

However, these brutal beasts could not triumph over the Jedi. Anakin used his Force powers to tame the reek enough to ride it. He charged it into the nexu, flattening it and saving Padmé. Obi-Wan managed to defend himself against the acklay's onslaught long enough for the clone army to arrive, led by Master Yoda.

GEONOSIS
ARENA BEAST

Prisoners on Geonosis were thrown into arenas with wild creatures that tried to destroy them for a crowd's entertainment. Obi-Wan Kenobi faced the vicious acklay but it was no match for the adept Jedi.

DEFENCE
Obi-Wan Kenobi used a Geonosian picador's pike to defend himself against the acklay's brutal onslaught.

DEADLY ATTACK
The acklay lives
underwater, but it
hunts for its prey on
land. The creature has
razor-sharp teeth for
cutting flesh and it
walks on the tips
of its long claws.

Utapau Clash

In a high-speed chase, the level of danger faced by the Jedi is even higher. On the rocky planet Utapau, Obi-Wan Kenobi would not let anything stop him from pursuing General Grievous. Their chase took them through the multilevel tunnels of Utapau's underground cities. Grievous rode his wheel bike, a deadly vehicle armed with a laser canon, while Obi-Wan rode on a varactyl lizard named Boga, which was more than capable of keeping pace with Grievous.

Obi-Wan dropped his lightsaber during the chase, but managed to grab Grievous's electrostaff. This powerful weapon emitted deadly levels of energy and was made of very strong material named phrik alloy that does not break – even after being struck by a lightsaber blade.

The enemies duelled as they rushed across Utapau's deep caverns. Grievous's heavy armour protected him from Obi-Wan's attacks, although the cyborg's armoured plates became loose in their brawl.

Obi-Wan used the Force to grab Grievous's pistol and blasted his opponent through a gap in his armour. Obi-Wan's fatal shot enflamed Grievous and destroyed him in an exploding ball of fire.

Battle of Wits

Not all battles are a straightforward case of pitting weaponry, skills and experience against the opposing side. Quick thinking can win a battle just as much as a superior spaceship can.

Luke Skywalker used his wits to survive

when a notorious crime lord called Jabba the Hutt captured Princess Leia, Han Solo and their loyal Wookiee ally, Chewbacca. Jabba was a slimy, gruesome gangster, but Luke was not afraid of him and demanded that the slug-like alien release his friends. Jabba didn't have to physically fight Luke – he had his own devious methods.

He dropped Luke into a rancor beast's den, but Luke's Jedi powers were so strong that he managed to trap the rancor. Jabba was not giving up yet. He ordered his guards to feed Luke and his friends to a tentacled creature named the Sarlacc. Cunningly, Luke had hidden his lightsaber inside his droid, R2-D2. R2-D2 ejected the lightsaber toward Luke who destroyed Jabba's men. Leia was quick-witted too, and this distraction gave her the chance to strangle Jabba with her prisoner's chains. Imprisoning friends of the Jedi would be Jabba the Hutt's last mistake!

JABBA'S GANG

Crime lord Jabba the Hutt and his evil crew did not have Force powers, but they still managed to spread chaos and corruption across the galaxy.

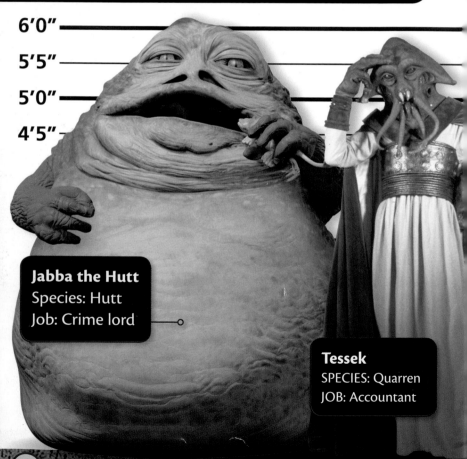

6'0"
5'5"
5'0"
4'5"

Jabba the Hutt
Species: Hutt
Job: Crime lord

Tessek
SPECIES: Quarren
JOB: Accountant

Ephant Mon
Species: Chevin
Job: Chief of security

Bib Fortuna
Species: Twi'lek
Job: Manager of
Jabba's palace

8'5"
8'0"
7'5"
7'0"

CELEBRATION
When the people of Naboo have something to celebrate, such as victory in battle, they hold a vibrant triumph parade.

A New Era

The reign of the Galactic Empire was brought to a close following the demise of Emperor Palpatine and Darth Vader, and the destruction of the second Death Star. Peace and justice were restored to the galaxy. The good news spread quickly and people across the galaxy rejoiced. Their lives were no longer threatened.

The Rebel Alliance established a New Republic to bring democracy to the galaxy. However, the galaxy's troubles were not completely resolved.

In the future, loyal Imperial officers would continue to attack the New Republic with surviving vehicles of the Imperial fleet. And hundreds of planets would have to be won over by the new

democratic rule. At that time, however, the Emperor had been defeated and fireworks lit up the sky in celebration high above the skyscrapers of Coruscant and across many other planets, too. For Luke Skywalker, Han Solo, Princess Leia and their friends, a new era had begun.

BATTLE ANALYSIS: NABOO

The Trade Federation, controlled by the Sith Lord Darth Sidious, invaded the planet Naboo to provoke a war. Queen Amidala and her allies led six dangerous missions to put an end to the invasion.

1. GRASS PLAINS

OBJECTIVE:
Gungans to create a diversion for the droid army.

OUTCOME:
Battle begins, droids are successfully distracted.

MISSION COMPLETE

2. THEED PALACE

OBJECTIVE:
Queen Amidala and her soldiers to sneak into the royal palace.

OUTCOME:
Team avoids battle droids and enters through window.

MISSION COMPLETE

3. SPACE BATTLE

OBJECTIVE:
Naboo starfighter pilots to destroy the Droid Control Ship.

....

OUTCOME:
Pilots engage hostile vulture droids, but suffer losses.

MISSION FAILED

4. JEDI VS SITH DUEL

OBJECTIVE:
Jedi to eliminate the Sith Darth Maul.

....

OUTCOME:
Obi-Wan defeats Maul, but Qui-Gon dies.

MISSION COMPLETE

5. THEED THRONE ROOM

OBJECTIVE:
Queen Amidala to capture the Trade Federation viceroy, Nute Gunray.

....

OUTCOME:
Queen outsmarts the viceroy and makes him surrender.

MISSION COMPLETE

6. DROID CONTROL SHIP DESTRUCTION

MISSION COMPLETE

OBJECTIVE:
Naboo pilots to destroy the Droid Control Ship.

OUTCOME:
Anakin Skywalker blows up the ship shutting down the droid army.

BATTLE ANALYSIS:
GEONOSIS

The Separatists – led by Count Dooku –
built a large droid army. When Obi-Wan Kenobi was
captured by Count Dooku, the Republic sent envoys
and troops to Geonosis to resolve the issue.

1. DROID FACTORY

OBJECTIVE:
Anakin Skywalker and Padmé
Amidala to rescue Obi-Wan Kenobi.

....

OUTCOME:
Anakin Skywalker and Padmé
Amidala are captured.

MISSION FAILED

2. EXECUTION ARENA

OBJECTIVE:
Anakin, Padmé and
Obi-Wan to escape
execution.

OUTCOME:
Captives survive and
destroy vicious beasts.

MISSION COMPLETE

3. JEDI STRIKE FORCE

OBJECTIVE:
Jedi team to rescue captives from droids.

. . . .

OUTCOME:
Many Jedi killed, Jedi survivors surrounded by droid army.

MISSION INCOMPLETE

4. ARRIVAL OF CLONE ARMY

OBJECTIVE:
Clone army to rescue survivors.

. . . .

OUTCOME:
Survivors airlifted out of arena.

MISSION COMPLETE

5. BATTLE OF GEONOSIS

OBJECTIVE:
Jedi to lead clone troopers and vehicles against droid army.

. . . .

OUTCOME:
Despite many fatalities during a full-scale battle, clone army is victorious.

MISSION COMPLETE

6. DUEL WITH DOOKU

OBJECTIVE:
Obi-Wan, Anakin and Yoda to prevent Count Dooku's escape from Geonosis.

OUTCOME:
Anakin loses his arm, Count Dooku escapes.

MISSION FAILED

BATTLE ANALYSIS:
YAVIN

The Emperor's Death Star tracked the rebels to their headquarters on Yavin 4. The Rebel Alliance only had one chance to destroy the powerful battle station and save themselves.

1. DEATH STAR APPROACH

OBJECTIVE:
Red and Gold Squadrons to weaken the Death Star's defences.

OUTCOME:
The Death Star's ion cannons and communications centres are taken out.

MISSION COMPLETE

2. SPACE BATTLE

OBJECTIVE:
Rebel pilots to wipe out Imperial TIE fighters.

OUTCOME:
During fast-paced combat both sides take losses.

MISSION FAILED

3. FIRST TRENCH RUN

OBJECTIVE:
Gold Squadron's Y-wings to hit the Death Star's thermal exhaust port.
....

OUTCOME:
Y-wings destroyed by Darth Vader.

MISSION FAILED

4. SECOND TRENCH RUN

OBJECTIVE:
Red Squadron's X-wings to hit the thermal exhaust port.
....

OUTCOME:
X-wings fire but miss, and are destroyed by Darth Vader.

MISSION FAILED

5. DARTH VADER

OBJECTIVE:
Millennium Falcon to attack Darth Vader.
....

OUTCOME:
Han Solo damages Vader's special TIE fighter, so Luke can fire at the Death Star's exhaust port.

MISSION COMPLETE

6. FINAL CHANCE

OBJECTIVE:
Luke Skywalker to destroy the Death Star.

OUTCOME:
Luke torpedoes the exhaust port, blowing up the Death Star.

MISSION COMPLETE

BATTLE ANALYSIS: ENDOR

The Rebel Alliance was on a mission to shut down the second Death Star. A strike team landed on Endor to demolish it. This report examines the events of the Battle on Endor.

1. CAPTURED

OBJECTIVE:
Han Solo, Princess Leia and Chewbacca to destroy the shield generator.

OUTCOME:
The trio realises they have walked into a trap and are captured.

MISSION FAILED

2. SPACE BATTLE

OBJECTIVE:
Rebels to elude Imperial warships near the Death Star.

OUTCOME:
Rebels destroy Imperial ships, but take heavy losses too.

MISSION INCOMPLETE

3. LAND BATTLE

OBJECTIVE:
Rebels to fight their way out of the Imperial trap.

OUTCOME:
Ewoks join the fight and beat the soldiers with spears and rocks.

MISSION COMPLETE

4. DEATH STAR DUEL

OBJECTIVE:
Luke Skywalker to defeat the Emperor.

OUTCOME:
Darth Vader throws the Emperor into a shaft to save Luke.

MISSION COMPLETE

5. SHIELD GENERATOR

OBJECTIVE:
Strike team to destroy the shield protecting the Death Star.

OUTCOME:
This time, the generator is blown up.

MISSION COMPLETE

6. DESTROY DEATH STAR

OBJECTIVE:
Lando to trigger an explosion in the Death Star's main reactor.

OUTCOME:
With the shield down, Lando blasts the core.

MISSION COMPLETE

Quiz

1. What was Yoda's rank in the Jedi Order?

2. The Trade Federation was run by which greedy aliens?

3. What power source is housed in the hilt of a Jedi's lightsaber?

4. How many members of the Jedi High Council were there?

5. Which brave pilot destroyed the Droid Control Ship?

6. Where did the land battle between the Gungan army and the Trade Federation army occur?

7. Which Jedi is said to have ordered the creation of a secret clone army?

8. To which planet did Yoda flee after his fight with Count Dooku?

9. What type of rifle did Boba Fett carry?

10. What was the length of a vulture droid?

11. The Rebel Alliance launched a space assault on the first Death Star from their base on which planet?

12. Where did Leia hide her message for Obi-Wan?

13. What type of beast did Luke Skywalker defeat inside Jabba's palace?

14. How many reactors were there on the second Death Star?

15. Which furry creatures helped the Rebel Alliance on the forest moon of Endor?

Glossary

Apprentice
A trainee or learner.

Bounty hunter
Someone who searches for and captures people for a reward.

Chancellor
The person who leads the government, known as the Senate.

Chasm
A deep hole.

Clone
An exact copy of something or someone.

Compassion
Sympathy for others.

Corporation
A group of businesses that have formed an organisation.

Cyborg
Someone who is part-living and part-robot.

Deflect
To block something coming towards you and force it in another direction.

Divert
To change the direction of something.

Empire
A group of nations or worlds ruled by one leader – the Emperor.

Galaxy
A group of millions of stars and planets.

Gloat
To be smug about something.

Goad
To deliberately anger and irritate someone.

Jedi
A group of beings who defend peace and justice in the galaxy.

Manipulate
To control or influence someone.

Reactor
A device in spaceships used to generate power for travel.

Repel
To force something back.

Republic
A nation, world or group of worlds in which people vote for their leaders.

Separatists
Those who oppose the Galactic Republic.

Sinkhole
A hole in the rock beneath a planet's surface.

Sith
Evil beings who use the dark side of the Force.

Underestimate
To not value someone's abilities highly enough.

Viceroy
An official who is a representative of the Emperor.

Wield
To handle a weapon or tool.

Quiz answers
1. Jedi Grand Master 2. Neimoidians 3. A crystal 4. 12 5. Anakin Skywalker
6. Great Grass Plains of Naboo 7. Jedi Master Sifo-Dyas 8. Dagobah
9. EE-3 carbine rifle 10. 6.96 m (22.75 ft) 11. Inside R2-D2 12. *Tantive IV*
13. A rancor 14. Three 15. Ewoks

Index

Guide for Parents

DK Reads is a three-level reading series for children, developing the habit of reading widely for both pleasure and information. These books have exciting running text interspersed with a range of reading genres to suit your child's reading ability, as required by the school curriculum. Each book is designed to develop your child's reading skills, fluency, grammar awareness and comprehension in order to build confidence and engagement when reading.

Ready for a *Reading Alone* book
YOUR CHILD SHOULD
- be able to read independently and silently for extended periods of time.
- read aloud flexibly and fluently, in expressive phrases with the listener in mind.
- respond to what they are reading with an enquiring mind.

A valuable and shared reading experience

Supporting children when they are reading proficiently can encourage them to value reading and to view reading as an interesting, purposeful and enjoyable pastime. So here are a few tips on how to use this book with your child.

TIP 1 Reading aloud as a learning opportunity:

- If your child has already read some of the book, ask him/her to explain the earlier part briefly.
- Encourage your child to read slightly slower than his/her normal silent reading speed so that the words are clear and the listener has time to absorb the information, too.

Reading aloud provides your child with practice in expressive reading and performing to a listener, as well as a chance to share his/her responses to the storyline and the information.

TIP 2 Praise, share and chat:

- Encourage your child to recall specific details after each chapter.

- Provide opportunities for your child to pick out interesting words and discuss what they mean.

- Discuss how the author captures the reader's interest, or how effective the non-fiction layouts are.

- Ask the questions provided on some pages and in the quiz. These help to develop comprehension skills and awareness of the language used.

- Ask if there's anything that your child would like to discover more about.

Further information can be researched in the index of other non-fiction book or on the internet.

A FEW ADDITIONAL TIPS

- Continue to read to your child regularly to demonstrate fluency, phrasing and expression; to find out or check information; and for sharing enjoyment.

- Encourage your child to read a range of different genres, such as newspapers, poems, review articles and instructions.

- Provide opportunities for your child to read to a variety of eager listeners, such as a sibling or a grandparent.

Here are some other
DK Reads you might enjoy.

Pony Club
Emma is so excited – she is going to
horse-riding camp with her older sister!

Terrors of the Deep
Marine biologists Dom and Jake take their
deep-sea submersible down into the deepest,
darkest ocean trenches in the world.

Star Wars™: Sith Wars
Meet the Sith Lords who are trying to take
over the galaxy. Discover their evil
plans and deadly armies.